CONFLICT IN SOUTHERN AFRICA

Chris Smith

Wayland

Conflicts

Titles in the series:
Conflict in Eastern Europe
Conflict in Southern Africa
Conflict in the Middle East
The Breakup of the Soviet Union

Cover: Zulus at a protest rally in Soweto, South Africa, in May 1991.

Title page: SWAPO supporters at a rally celebrating the return to Namibia of SWAPO leaders, in June 1989.
In November of the same year SWAPO won Namibia's first elections.

Picture acknowledgements
The publishers would like to thank the following for supplying their photographs for use as illustrations in this book: Camera Press 16 (Adespoton); ET Archive 4 (Charles Fripp), 9 (Africana Museum); Mary Evans Picture Library 7; International Defence and Aid Fund for Southern Africa 14 *bottom*, 15 (Tony McGrath); Link 21 *both* (Greg English), 24 (Greg English), 26 (Greg English), 30 (Trevor Samson), 31 (Orde Eliason), 38 (Orde Eliason), 41 (Orde Eliason), 42 (Orde Eliason), 43 (Orde Eliason); Oxfam 27 (Keith Bernstein), 34 (Keith Bernstein), 35 (Akwe Amosa); Popperfoto 6, 29 (A Gordon); Reportage 39 (Carlos Guarita), 44 (Carlos Guarita); Rex Features *cover* (Mark Peters/ Sipa Press),10 (Sipa Press), 14 *top* (IDAF/Sipa Press), 18 (Maggie Steber/Sipa Press), 20 (P Frilet/ Sipa Press), 22 (Habib/Sipa Press), 25 (Jim Hooper), 28 (Johan Kuus), 32 (Durand/Sipa Press), 33 (Sipa Press), 36 (Laif), 37 (Durand/Sipa); Topham Picture Library *title page* (Adil Bradlow), 5 (Adil Bradlow), 12 (Associated Press), 13 (Associated Press), 19, 23, 40 (Associated Press), 45 (Adil Bradlow).
The maps on pages 8, 11 and 17 were supplied by Peter Bull.

Series editor: William Wharfe
Designer/Typesetter: Malcolm Walker/Kudos Editorial and Design Services

First published in 1992 by
Wayland (Publishers) Ltd
61 Western Road, Hove
East Sussex BN3 1JD

British Library Cataloguing in Publication Data
Smith, Chris
  Conflict in Southern Africa. – (Conflicts Series)
  I. Title II. Series
  968.06

ISBN 0-7502-0357-9

Printed in Italy by G. Canale & C.S.p.A., Turin

Contents

CHAPTER 1

INTRODUCTION

Southern Africa, which comprises the Republic of South Africa and its neighbours, has long been an area of poverty, conflict and despair. There are many reasons for conflict in the region, and most of them are linked to the fact that the area was colonized by Europeans from the seventeenth century onwards.

The Europeans brought their money and technology, but they were in no hurry to share the wealth they accumulated in South Africa with the local population. The peoples who were living in Southern Africa before the Europeans arrived found themselves forced to fight to retain their land. By the end of the nineteenth century, the Europeans controlled almost all of Africa, and although some degree of democracy was a feature of most European nations, they rarely granted this to their colonies.

During the twentieth century, and particularly after the Second World War, Africans fought to free themselves from the control of the colonists. By 1990, all the countries in Africa achieved independence. However, independence has not necessarily solved problems.

Some countries had substantial, well-

The Battle of Isandhlwana in 1879, between the British and Zulus. The British lost this battle, but went on to defeat the Zulu king, Cetshwayo.

25 October 1990: police fire on demonstrators in Khayalitsha, near Cape Town in South Africa. One of the demonstrators was shot dead. Such an event was typical of the conflict between South Africa's government and its opponents.

established European populations – South Africa in particular. When it declared itself independent, in 1926, about a fifth of the population of South Africa was white. Most of the white population had no intention of allowing the non-Europeans the right to vote. Controlled by the whites, the government of South Africa became a bastion of white power in Africa. To protect itself, the government set up a system of laws in the 1950s, enforced by harsh policing, to prevent blacks, Asians and coloureds (people of mixed race) from seizing power. The new laws also prevented them from sharing equally with the whites the wealth that the country could produce.

The stance of the whites in South Africa has created years of conflict and violence within the country. In addition, it has affected South Africa's relations with its neighbours, which are all now run by governments with a majority of black representatives. So far, this has not led to a full-scale war between the two sides. However, there

have been numerous occasions when South Africa has attempted to create and encourage instability in the region, to prevent its opponents becoming strong enough to mount a threat.

But for the existence of this minority government the prospects for peace and development would be increased considerably. True, there might still be problems between and within countries but, without doubt, a large proportion of the conflict in Southern Africa can be traced directly to the white minority government in South Africa.

The following chapters look at the history of conflict in Southern Africa, from the arrival of the Europeans to the more recent battles (both political and military) between South Africa and its neighbouring countries. In the early 1990s South Africa's white government seemed to be set on the path of reform – the final chapter considers the chances for peace in Southern Africa, in the shadow of past conflicts.

COLONIZATION, CONFLICT AND CONTROL

Written records of human activity in Southern Africa only go back to the arrival of European traders on the southern tip of Africa (the Cape of Good Hope) from the fifteenth century onwards. But archaeological evidence shows that there were San, Khoi-khoi and Nguni peoples living throughout the area that is today the Republic of South Africa, before the arrival of Europeans.

The Europeans arrived in the form of Dutch settlers. Holland was one of the most powerful European trading nations of the seventeenth century. In 1652, the Dutch East India Company set up a supply station at the Cape of Good Hope for the ships travelling to and from the East Indies, mainly Indonesia. The Dutch gradually enlarged the small settlement into a permanent colony – the Cape Colony – forcing the local people (the Khoi-khoi) to move away, or to work on the colony's farms as slaves. In 1806, with Holland overrun by Napoleon, the British occupied Cape Colony on the basis that any Dutch settlement outside Europe was an acceptable target.

British control of the colony was made permanent in 1814, when the Dutch government handed over Cape Colony to the British for a settlement of £6 million. In 1834 the British abolished slave labour – on which the Dutch farmers depended. To get away from British rule, between 1836 and 1840, the Dutch farmers

During the Great Trek (1836-40) about 14,000 Boers emigrated from Cape Colony.

This drawing shows a South African diamond mine in 1872. Black workers suffered harsh working conditions and often brutal treatment at the hands of British and Boer bosses.

known as Boers trekked north across the plains and set up new independent states beyond the River Orange and the River Vaal.

As the British colony expanded, the Boers were forced to move further inland. This created clashes with the Bantu-speaking peoples, including the Zulus, who had moved south in the previous century. A three-way conflict resulted, between the Boers, the British and the indigenous peoples.

The British were particularly concerned because Cape Town and Simonstown (in Cape Colony) were important ports on the sea route to their colonial possessions in the East, especially India. The British were keen to prevent the Boers from trading from other ports in South Africa, although this threat diminished once the Suez Canal opened (1869), which gave Britain a more direct access to its eastern colonies (see map on page 8). Also, a major factor was the British desire to control the newly discovered diamond

and gold fields in the Boer territories of the Orange Free State and Transvaal. The result was a concerted effort in the 1860s and 1870s by the British to expand to the north and close down any potential competition in the region. Inevitably, this led to the Boer War (1899-1902), during which the British government achieved the supremacy it required.

In the years immediately after the Boer War, British government policy in the Cape Colony changed to allow a partnership with the Boers, albeit an unequal one. However, little was given

In 1911 South Africa was home to nearly 6 million people. Of these, 4.02 million (67.3 per cent) were black, 1.28 million (21.4 per cent) were white, 520,000 (8.7 per cent) were Coloured and 150,000 (2.5 per cent) were Asians (mostly people who had migrated from India and Indonesia).

Source: 1911 Official South African Population Census

to the indigenous population – the San, Khoi-khoi and the Bantu-speaking peoples. In 1910 the separate Boer republics, Transvaal and Orange Free State, were brought into the Union of South Africa.

White domination of South Africa

From the very beginning of Dutch settlement in Southern Africa, Boers tried to keep themselves separate from non-Europeans. The first Dutch settlers had planted a hedge around their

Like the rest of Africa, Southern Africa was divided up into colonies by the major European powers.

encampment and had forbidden the indigenous peoples, the Khoi-khoi and San, from entering. With the creation of the Union of South Africa, the Boers – who now preferred the term 'Afrikaners' – were able to influence the way in which the whole of South Africa was governed. Although the British South Africans favoured giving rights (such as the vote) to an élite class of black South Africans, the attitude towards the majority of blacks was very different. Black Africans were seen as a source of cheap labour.

The Union of South Africa was made up of four areas. In the former British colonies of Natal and the Cape, white men and literate, property-

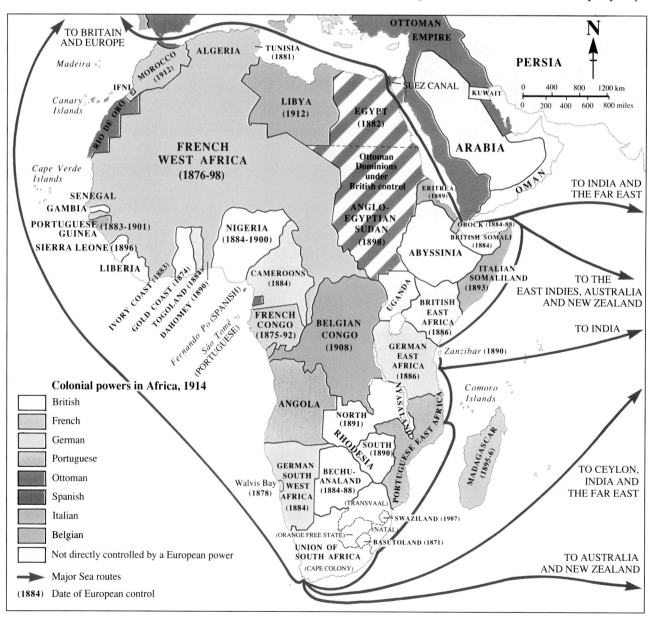

Black and Chinese workers built the South African railways. These men are shown working on the Delagoa Bay line, connecting the Mozambican port of Maputo with South African cities and mines.

owning or wealthy male blacks retained the right to vote. However, in the former Boer republics of Orange Free State and the Transvaal, no black person had a vote. But the majority of people in the new South African state were not white, which meant that a very small percentage of the population elected the government which passed laws affecting everybody.

In 1912 the African National Congress (ANC) was founded by a group of black tribal chiefs, intellectuals and Christian ministers, to campaign for rights for blacks, in particular the vote for all black, Coloured and Asian people. They believed all South African people should see themselves as one nation rather than as a collection of separate tribes. Their policy was to win a place for the black African in South African society through peaceful negotiation.

The majority of white politicians, however, were more interested in removing the few rights that remained for non-white people. In 1913 the Natives' Land Act divided South Africa into areas for whites and areas for non-whites. As a result, in the Transvaal and Orange Free State, hundreds of thousands of non-whites were evicted from farms, or forced to work for white farmers. From 1922 onwards, the government passed a series of acts intended to stop non-whites moving into white areas.

Coloureds and Asians in South Africa
South Africa's Coloured population's roots go back to the seventeenth and eighteenth centuries to children born of white colonists and Malay women slaves (from the Dutch East Indies), white colonists and Khoi-khoi and San women, and also of Malay slave men and Khoi-khoi and San women. Today, most Coloureds live in Cape Province.

Since the middle of the nineteenth century there has been an Asian population in South Africa. These were from India, brought in the 1860s by the British to work on the sugar plantations of Natal. There are also people of Chinese origin, whose ancestors were employed to build railways for the British in South Africa at the turn of the century.

APARTHEID

In 1939, at the start of the Second World War, South Africa's Prime Minister, General Jan Smuts, committed the country to the side of the Allies against the Germans and Italians. Yet, many Afrikaners had more sympathy with Germany than with Britain – the old enemy. As a direct result, Smuts' United Party lost popularity and in 1948 lost the election narrowly to the National Party under the leadership of Dr D F Malan.

As part of his election campaign, Dr Malan had talked a lot about keeping the races in South Africa as separate as possible. For instance, the National Party manifesto stated: 'National policy must be so designed that it advances the ideal of ultimate separation on a natural basis.' Dr Malan used a special Afrikaans word to describe racial separation, 'apartheid', which means 'apartness'. Since then the word 'apartheid' has been used to describe all the laws passed and actions taken to separate the races in South Africa.

In the late 1940s and early 1950s the National Party looked for ways of promoting apartheid. One of the most important laws passed in this period was the Group Areas Act (1950). The Act set out areas which could be occupied only by people of a particular racial group. Entire black and coloured populations were moved to townships outside the cities, and the areas where they had lived were given over to whites. The 1953 Reservation of Separate Amenities Act ordered that all public facilities such as swimming pools, beaches, parks, toilets, trains, buses etc were now allowed to have separate sections for whites and for blacks.

In 1952 a new pass was issued to all black and coloured South African men, which had to be carried at all times. Some black and coloured people, mostly those working for whites, were allowed to stay in white areas, but otherwise they were allowed to stay for no more than three days. The passes were used by the government to enforce the Group Areas Act, and, from 1953 onwards, the Bantu Authorities Act, which set up more than 260 'tribal reserves' or 'homelands' which were allocated to the main tribal groups (such as Tswana, Zulu or Xhosa).

The land in each homeland was often poor and at best could support about half of the population,

Under apartheid, non-whites were told and shown clearly where they could and could not eat.

which had swollen as a direct result of the apartheid laws. Consequently, many of the people became dependent upon white-owned farms and industries (usually located just outside the homelands). The apartheid laws had been successful in creating a plentiful supply of cheap labour for white-owned factories, mines and farms. However, so that working-class whites were not put out of employment, the government passed the Industrial Conciliation Act (1956), which made it possible to reserve certain jobs for particular racial groups. For instance, in Cape Town, only whites could be ambulance drivers, firemen, or traffic policemen above the rank of constable. Also, black and coloured workers could not go on strike – as stated by a law passed in 1953.

One of the key apartheid laws was the 1953 Bantu Education Act. On presenting the Act to Parliament, Dr Hendrik Verwoerd, the Minister for Bantu Affairs, said: 'There is no place for the Bantu [a black person] in the European

community above certain forms of labour ... for that reason it is of no avail [use] for him to receive a training which has as its aim absorption in the European community.' So the Act declared that all black schoolchildren should be encouraged to do manual work rather than preparing any of them for more highly paid skilled jobs reserved for whites.

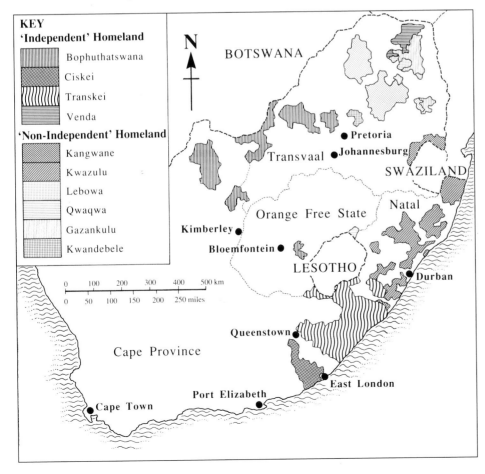

The homelands, or Bantustans, that were set up from 1953 onwards by the Bantu Authorities Act. By 1981, Transkei, Bophuthatswana, Venda and Ciskei were all made 'independent' states. However, their independence was not recognized outside South Africa and they remained economically and politically dependent on South Africa.

21 March 1960: police survey the scene in Sharpeville immediately after opening fire on demonstrators. Sixty-seven people were killed. Many of them were shot in the back.

Reaction to apartheid

Few non-whites had the opportunity to make their views on apartheid known by voting. In 1959 the white-dominated Parliament voted to remove representatives of Africans from Parliament. From that point the only non-whites represented were coloureds in Cape Province, who elected just four, white, members of the House of Assembly out of a total of 160.

Large-scale opposition to the apartheid system came with the Defiance Campaign in 1952, organized by the ANC and the Indian Congress (the campaigning organization set up by the Asian community in South Africa). The campaign involved hundreds of volunteers deliberately breaking the segregation laws. This was followed in 1955 by the formation of the Congress Alliance. Following the opening meeting of the Congress Alliance, the Freedom Charter was drawn up, calling for a non-racial democracy and equal opportunities in education and employment. Despite arrests of the leaders of the Congress Movement, peaceful protests continued.

Sharpeville

On 21 March 1960 anti-pass law demonstrations were organized by the ANC and the new, radical, Pan-Africanist Congress (PAC). Robert Sobukwe, the PAC leader, was arrested. On the same day a crowd gathered around Sharpeville police station, also protesting against the pass laws. The police fired upon the crowd, injuring 360 people and killing sixty-seven. According to hospital testimonies many were shot in the back. Following this event the ANC and PAC were both banned and they both decided to turn to armed conflict. The ANC's new military section was named *Umkhonto we Sizwe*, or Spear of the Nation, the PAC's armed unit was called *Poqo*, or We Go Alone.

News of the Sharpeville shootings shocked people around the world. Within weeks of the shootings foreign companies withdrew about £750 million of investment from South Africa. In 1962 the United Nations (UN) requested its members to break off all diplomatic and most commercial relations with South Africa. In 1963

> '. . . what we want is a society where the individual matters, and not the colour of his skin, or the shape of his nose. Racial group privileges or discriminations are incompatible with this. The policies of apartheid now being practised in the Union of South Africa are a daily affront to this belief in individual human dignity. . .' Julius Nyerere, Prime Minister of Tanzania, writing in the *Observer* newspaper during the Commonwealth Heads of Government conference in March 1961.

the UN Security Council recommended that all UN members cease selling arms to South Africa.

Much of the rise in international concern came about because a large number of African states gained their independence in the 1960s (see Chapter 4). As new states they joined the General Assembly of the UN, cast their votes as independent states and stood on various committees which provided the opportunity for them to voice their concerns. Together with other developing, or 'Third World', nations these states also made up the Non-Aligned Movement of some seventy or more countries which acted as a powerful voting group within the UN. Many of

these countries were also members of the Commonwealth, which in March 1961 voted to exclude South Africa because of apartheid. The South African government responded by declaring itself a Republic in May 1961, severing all ties with the Commonwealth.

However, the efforts of the UN were enormously weakened by certain countries, amongst others, Britain and the USA, which held then (as now) powerful positions within the UN. Both refused to accept that South Africa posed a threat to international peace and security, despite the simmering tensions in the region and growing evidence that South Africa was developing nuclear weapons. In addition, there were powerful British and American business interests which stood to lose a great deal if the West accepted all the UN recommendations.

Order by force
Meanwhile, in South Africa the government issued a series of laws designed to impose order. Public meetings were banned and restrictions were put on the press. Police were allowed to hold people for ninety days if they were suspected of being involved in anti-government activities.

The pass book which all black South Africans were forced to carry after 1952. The pass books were used to help police enforce the 1950 Group Areas Act, which set out where people of different 'races' (black, Coloured, Asian or white) were allowed to live. Hundreds of thousands of people were arrested each year for pass book offences. The pass laws were finally abolished in 1986 (see page 30).

Nelson Mandela
One of the key figures in the ANC was a black lawyer – Nelson Mandela. He had founded the Youth League of the ANC and was arrested for his part in the Defiance Campaign in 1952. He was released but in 1956 was arrested again for high treason. In 1960 he was acquitted, and after Sharpeville he helped to form *Umkhonto we Sizwe*. In 1962 he was arrested after travelling abroad, and while in prison, new evidence was produced for which he was sentenced to life imprisonment in 1964 (for 'sabotage' and 'conspiracy to overthrow the government by revolution'). Mandela was released, after a prolonged international campaign, in 1990 (see page 30).

Under the Terrorism Act of 1967, suspected terrorists could be held indefinitely without trial. The security forces used the law to detain many people, even when there was no apparent reason to suspect them of terrorist activity. The harsh measures restored an appearance of order, and foreign investment returned.

Problems with apartheid in the 1970s

In the early 1970s South African industry underwent a series of changes which led to a greater demand for skilled labour. Black workers began to use the bargaining power this gave them. Although their unions were not recognized by the government, they still managed to organize themselves effectively and, in 1973, there was a series of massive strikes. As a result, wages went up and the job reservation programme for whites was relaxed. The government recognized unions, thinking that it could deal with the black labour force more effectively that way, and took some steps towards improving education and training for blacks. Yet, no steps were taken towards dismantling the apartheid system.

With the ANC and PAC banned, a new student-based political movement became prominent in the early 1970s. The Black Consciousness movement aimed to give black and Asian people pride in their history and their identity – in an attempt to work against the feeling of being second-class citizens in the apartheid system which favoured whites. A key figure in this movement was Steve Biko, founder-member of the South African Students Organization (SASO). After a SASO rally in 1975 celebrating the Marxist victory in Mozambique (see page 21), nine of the student leaders were arrested and later convicted as 'terrorists'.

The first of 360 deaths during the Soweto riots in 1976.

One view of apartheid South Africa in the 1970s. The white child has a nanny to look after her, the black child sells ice-cream on the street. Anger at the poor quality of education offered to black children sparked off the Soweto riots in 1976.

Soweto

On 16 June 1976 10,000 schoolchildren demonstrated in the township of Soweto. They were protesting against the introduction of Afrikaans as one of the two languages of school instruction. It was felt that Afrikaans was the language of the white government, and that to add a third language of instruction (in addition to their own tribal language and English) would only make the chance of a good education even more remote. When the police used force aginst the protesting children, riots broke out, lasting for three weeks. The official figures eventually revealed that 360 blacks had been killed during the riots – the true figure may have been higher.

The government's reaction to the riots was to impose ever tighter security. During 1977 the security forces imposed major restrictions on black organizations (all Black Consciousness groups were banned) and arrested many more black leaders, including Steve Biko who died in detention from injuries he received during interrogation. Eventually, the government made small concessions – electricity for the townships and no legal requirement to teach Afrikaans in schools.

Soweto reawakened foreign public opposition to apartheid. The anti-apartheid campaign outside South Africa called for severe economic sanctions to be imposed, especially by the European Community and the USA, the aim being to isolate and weaken the white government, force it to abolish apartheid and give the vote to everyone over eighteen.

By 1980 many of the apartheid laws had been in place for over twenty-five years. The majority of people in South Africa – the blacks, coloureds and, to a lesser extent, the Asians – had suffered terrible poverty and repression. The South African economy had suffered from job reservation (which prevented jobs being awarded on merit), a poorly educated and inadequately trained workforce, strikes, sabotage, some economic sanctions and a growing nervousness on the part of foreign investors.

Apartheid also affected South Africa's relations with its neighbouring countries. The term 'front-line states' was, in a sense, created by apartheid policies: the South African border became the 'front line' between the state that created apartheid and those – across the border – which openly opposed it. The first group of front-line states were: Tanzania, Zambia, Angola, Mozambique; they were joined by Zimbabwe (1980) and Namibia (1989) after they became independent.

BEYOND SOUTH AFRICA'S BORDERS

South Africa is both the dominant state in Southern Africa and the central influence upon the region's recent history. However, each country has its own story, and before we can understand how conflict has affected Southern Africa we need to look briefly at each one in turn.

Although the Dutch were the first Europeans to make a major impact upon the region, they were not the first to arrive. The Portuguese landed on the west coast of Africa in 1483, and it would be a full four centuries before they agreed to independence for their colony of Angola. However, Portuguese settlement in Angola did not begin in earnest until 1945, immediately after the Second World War. As Portugal became an increasingly poor country, with the lowest living standards in Western Europe, some 400,000 white people migrated to Angola between 1945 and 1965. They believed that they would be better off in Africa than in rural Portugal. When this proved to be true they rigidly rejected any move by the black Angolans to challenge their economic well-being and political status.

The Portuguese were also present in south-east Africa, having established forts and churches on the coast of Mozambique in the sixteenth century. Portuguese settlers did not arrive in large numbers until the 1950s, just prior to the war of independence which began in 1960.

A Portuguese officer in Mozambique in 1973, preparing troops for a raid against Frelimo rebels.

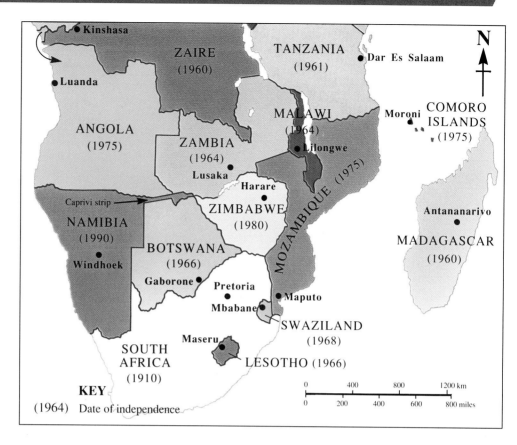

This map shows the states of Southern Africa after all of them had acquired independence. The date that each country became independent is shown in brackets. By 1980, Namibia and South Africa were the only states in Southern Africa that were controlled by a whites-only government.

Towards the end of the nineteenth century the major colonial powers – Britain, France, Germany, Belgium, Italy – competed against each other in what became known as the 'scramble for Africa' (see map on page 8). During this period, in 1890, South West Africa (Namibia) was brought under German control. The German colonists ran this barren region with an iron fist. On one occasion, when the Germans put down an uprising by the indigenous Bantu Herero people, 80,000 of them were killed. This was followed by an equally savage onslaught against the other indigenous group, the Nama, which nearly killed off the entire Nama people. By 1907 the indigenous people who had survived were little more than slaves to the German farmers.

During the First World War (1914-18), South West Africa was occupied by the South African armed forces. When Germany lost the war in Europe it was deprived of all its colonial possessions and South Africa was put in control of South West Africa by the League of Nations, the organization which preceded the United Nations. The League of Nations, set up after the First World War to help secure world peace, had required South Africa to make various improvements in South West Africa – including instituting freedom of religion and an end to alcohol, gun and slave trafficking. In fact, the South African Government merely took over where the Germans had left off. They drafted in white farmers to work the land, and the farmers set up their own parliament.

In the 1890s the British government had feared that the Germans and Boers would link up and block communications and connections to other parts of Africa controlled by the British. In addition to South West Africa, Germany controlled German East Africa (now known as Tanzania). In fact, Britain succeeded in extending its control far to the north to include areas that are now Zimbabwe, Zambia and Malawi. Success for Britain was primarily due to Cecil Rhodes, of the British South Africa Company. Rhodes became notorious for the extremely questionable means he used, which almost certainly amounted to cheating the African chiefs.

In 1923 Southern Rhodesia, eventually Zimbabwe, became an area of white settlement and a self-governing colony. In 1930 European settlers, who constituted 20 per cent of the population of Southern Rhodesia, were given in excess of 50 per cent of the land and all the towns. Salisbury (now Harare) developed into a wealthy city. Black Africans were barred from owning land in these areas. After the Second World War (1939-45) a large number of whites moved into the colony, especially from Britain. For a brief period (1953-63) Southern Rhodesia entered into an unsteady federation with Northern Rhodesia (Zambia) and Nyasaland (Malawi), areas which had also been brought under British control by Cecil Rhodes.

Independence

The Second World War was a turning-point in the history of Southern Africa. Most of the colonial powers, except Portugal, had been involved one way or another in this long and draining conflict. During the war, Britain had been forced to bow to the rising tide of Indian nationalism under the leadership of Mahatma Gandhi, whose first political experience came as a civil rights campaigner in South Africa. India successfully managed to acquire independence in 1947, a development which convinced many other African and Asian states that the system of colonialism was growing weaker. In addition, people in the colonies were becoming increasingly combative in their demands for independence. They demanded the right to determine their own political and economic futures and there were groups in Western Europe which argued strongly that the system of colonialism should be dismantled.

From Rhodesia to Zimbabwe

Independence for Rhodesia came in three distinct phases. First, Rhodesia became a self-governing colony in 1923. However, in practice the British government was only prepared to allow independence for the white population and kept the right to stop laws being passed which applied specifically to the African population. By the

1960s this situation had created problems. While black Rhodesians saw their northern neighbours (Northern Rhodesia/Zambia) being given independence, they were faced with a white government which was unwilling to accept any guidance from Britain on how independence might be brought about.

The second phase came to a head in 1965 when the white minority in Rhodesia declared UDI – a Unilateral Declaration of Independence. In addition to wanting complete freedom from British interference, the white minority was also influenced by events across the border in South Africa and the movement towards a full system of apartheid.

The third phase began after UDI when the black population of Rhodesia realized that their

Before the 1980 elections in Rhodesia/Zimbabwe, rebel troops joined government forces to help keep the peace. These former guerrillas were part of a new unit called 'Spear of the Nation'.

> 'I cannot see in my lifetime that the Africans will be sufficiently mature and reasonable to take over. . . If we ever have an African majority in this country we will have failed in our policy, because our policy is one of trying to make a place for the white man.' Ian Smith, shortly after becoming Prime Minister of Rhodesia, 1964.

chances of gaining the type of independence being granted to other African countries was extremely slim. In 1961 Joshua Nkomo founded the Zimbabwe African People's Union (ZAPU) and in 1963 his lieutenant, the Reverend Ndabaningi Sithole, broke away to form a more radical party, the Zimbabwe African National Union (ZANU). Once Prime Minister Ian Smith had declared UDI, his position became more rigid and a military clash between blacks and whites soon followed.

After UDI, Britain attempted to apply economic sanctions against Rhodesia, especially to prevent oil supplies, but the country was supplied by BP and Shell oil companies from South Africa, so no great impact was made. Between 1965 and 1972 the Rhodesian government was successful in containing the guerrilla tactics of both ZAPU and ZANU, until direct attacks began on remote white farms. Although the government attempted to react in the same way as its neighbour in South Africa, the guerrilla groups finally gained a prominent position and took the war closer to the capital, Salisbury. It was an extremely bitter conflict and led to tens of thousands of deaths and awful massacres and atrocities on both sides. Despite raids upon guerrilla camps in Zambia and newly independent Mozambique, it soon became apparent that the Rhodesian armed forces could not win the war. By 1975 it became clear that the white Rhodesian government would have to accede to black majority rule at some point. It set up a mixed-race government in 1979, but that proved unacceptable to the main opposition groups. Finally, in 1980, elections saw ZANU's Robert Mugabe become leader of the newly named Zimbabwe.

Robert Mugabe campaigning during Zimbabwe's elections in February 1980. Mugabe's ZANU party won fifty-seven of the eighty seats allocated to blacks.

Namibia

In South West Africa, renamed Namibia in 1968, black Africans were less successful in gaining independence. Despite the best intentions of the UN, the South African government refused to end its occupation. The South West Africa People's Organization (SWAPO) had been fighting the South African armed forces with guerilla warfare since 1966, but it was an uneven struggle, with the South African troops being some of the best equipped in the world. At one point there were tens of thousands of troops under South African control in Namibia. The South African government remained committed to maintain forces in Namibia because of the 78,000 white settlers they were unwilling to abandon and the country's rich mineral resources.

Having troops in Namibia also allowed South Africa to mount operations against other front-line states from the Caprivi Strip in northern Namibia (see map on page 17), where it had established military bases.

Independence did finally come to Namibia. In late 1988 South Africa agreed to talks over a peaceful settlement to the troubles in Namibia and Angola. One positive result was an agreement to implement UN Resolution 435, which called for the peaceful transition to Namibian independence, in exchange for the removal of Cuban troops in Angola, sent there to assist the MPLA government forces against the UNITA rebels (Cuba, being a communist-controlled country, had supported the communist MPLA against the US/South African-backed UNITA – see page 21).

On 21 March 1990 Namibia became an independent state, a remarkable outcome considering South Africa's previous policies towards the region. As expected, SWAPO won the November 1989 election, although not by

'We are Namibians and not South Africans. We do not now, and will not in the future, recognize your right to govern us; to make laws in which we have no say; to treat our country as if it were your property and as if you were our masters ... Only when South Africa realizes this and acts upon it, will it be possible for us to stop our struggle for freedom and justice in the land of our birth.' Toivo ja Toivo, SWAPO leader, speaking in court after being convicted for treason in 1968.

quite the expected margin. However, in order to begin to understand how and why the South African government changed its policy so dramatically, we need to look at South African politics from 1980 onwards (Chapter 6).

Angola

The Portuguese government was also unwilling to give up its colonies in Southern Africa. In Angola, the lure of coffee, diamonds, iron ore and oil was too great for Portugal, which was, in

Namibian SWAPO supporters at an independence rally in October, 1989.

the 1950s, becoming an increasingly poor nation. However, the black nationalists were badly affected by divisions amongst themselves and this greatly hampered their ability to mount a military campaign for independence.

In 1974 Portugal suffered a military coup and the country's dictator, Marcallo Caetano, was replaced by General Antonio de Spinola, who immediately took steps to end the war and grant Angola independence. Unfortunately, the independence movement could not maintain what little cohesion existed. Disputes over who would inherit power and differences in ideology created divisions which led to a power struggle between three main groups – the MPLA, FNLA and UNITA. Although independence was achieved in 1975, and the MPLA took power, this

was to be a new chapter rather than an end to violence in Angola.

Mozambique

After a ten-year struggle Mozambique gained independence from Portugal in June 1975. Victory for the independence movement was more straightforward than in Angola. This was because there was just one main rebel group – Frelimo – led at first by the capable Eduardo Mondlane who was assassinated in 1969, and then by Samora Machel. Frelimo was supported and supplied with arms from international sources including countries elsewhere in Africa. Although it is likely that Frelimo would have been successful anyway, the 1974 coup in Portugal aided the rebels.

(Inset) Samora Machel, President of Mozambique from 1969 until he died in a plane crash in 1986. Some have claimed that the plane was shot down by South African agents. (Main picture) Frelimo troops at Machel's funeral. Since independence in 1975, Frelimo forces have been fighting South African-supplied Renamo guerrillas.

December 1975: teenage FNLA rebels on patrol in Angola. Almost immediately after independence, in November 1975, civil war broke out in Angola between the MPLA based in Luanda, the FNLA based in Zaire and UNITA based in southern Angola.

Zambia

During the period of federation between Northern Rhodesia, Southern Rhodesia, and Nyasaland political opposition and unrest increased in Northern Rhodesia under two main rival groups. Independence from Britain followed relatively quickly (in 1964) and the country was renamed Zambia. As leader of the United National Independence Party (UNIP), Kenneth Kuanda became the first President.

Malawi

Like Northern Rhodesia, Nyasaland had less difficulty than its southern neighbours in attaining independence (in July 1964), chiefly because it is both extremely overpopulated and lacking in natural resources, which gave Britain little incentive to retain the colony. Renamed Malawi, the country's economy was in an appalling state when it became independent. There were limited options for development and many people began to seek employment in other countries, notably South Africa.

Botswana

When, in 1926, South Africa's Prime Minister Hertzog declared full independence, Britain kept control of Bechuanaland (see map on page 8). The area remained a British Protectorate until it was given independence in March 1965 and became a full member of the Commonwealth, taking the name of Botswana in 1966. Since then it has attempted to remain apart from the ongoing struggle between South Africa and the front-line states. Botswana is not desperately poor but it is extremely vulnerable. A very large proportion of its population relies upon work in South Africa. The railway, its economic lifeline, is jointly operated by Zimbabwe and South Africa.

Lesotho

In the early 1840s King Moshoeshoe I led his people into the mountains away from the advancing Boers. He conceded to the Boers the rich farmland of the Orange Free State and eventually asked Britain to assume responsibility for his tiny kingdom – Lesotho. Lesotho finally became independent in 1966, but it is surrounded by South Africa and there has been little

opportunity for the government of Lesotho to take any action that is really independent of South Africa.

Swaziland

Swaziland is the second smallest country in the whole of Africa. But for a short stretch of border shared with Mozambique it is surrounded by South Africa. Though independent, Swaziland is governed by a monarch, whose powers are set out in the country's constitution. Because Swaziland is so vulnerable it has been forced, like Lesotho and Botswana, to avoid a confrontation with South Africa. At the same time, however, Swazi leaders have attempted to avoid criticism from South Africa's enemies and possible isolation.

This demonstration greeted British Prime Minister Harold Macmillan on his visit to Blantyre, Nyasaland in January 1960. One of the posters asks 'Mac is Dr Banda with you?'. When Nyasaland gained independence in 1964, it was renamed Malawi and Dr Hastings Banda became prime minister. In July 1966 Malawi became a republic and Banda was elected president. He was made president for life in 1971.

CHAPTER 5

DESTABILIZATION AND 'TOTAL STRATEGY'

By the late 1970s all of South Africa's neighbours had attained independence, except Namibia. Faced with neighbouring governments that were openly hostile to white minority rule and apartheid, the South African government opted for a policy of continuous destabilization in the region, for four reasons. First, to tie up neighbours in internal problems, which would reduce their ability to consider regional problems. Second, to damage the transport lines and other services vital to the economies of landlocked countries – Malawi, Zambia and Zimbabwe – which would force these countries to trade through South Africa. Third, to prevent them from helping the ANC. Fourth, to demonstrate South Africa's power as a deterrent to weaker states.

> **Southern African Development Coordination Conference (SADCC)**
> Founded in 1980 on the eve of Zimbabwe's independence, the SADCC was set up by Angola, Botswana, Lesotho, Malawi, Mozambique, Swaziland, Tanzania, Zambia and Zimbabwe. The aim was for the member countries to work together to reduce their reliance on the South African economy. Working against South Africa's 'total strategy', the SADCC has tried to improve railways and roads between member countries so that imports and exports do not have to go through South Africa.

By the mid-1980s the policy of destabilization had been only partially successful. Consequently, in a bid to link internal economic and political problems, such as strikes, and pressures from neighbours, the government devised a policy known as 'total strategy', which was designed to counter what was seen as a total onslaught from communist groups backed by the Soviet Union.

From Namibia, South Africa was able to mount a campaign of destabilization against Angola. In 1975, South Africa attempted an invasion when Angola was at the point of independence. South African forces advanced almost as far as the capital, Luanda, far to the north. They were only stopped by the rapid dispatch of Cuban troops to Angola to assist the group in power – the MPLA. During the 1980s the conflict between South Africa and Angola intensified into a savage conventional war involving tank battles, widespread destruction and the involvement of thousands of troops on both sides, one example being the battle for Cuito Cuanavale.

However, South African involvement did not

UNITA troops in Southern Angola. The poster behind them shows UNITA leader Jonas Savimbi.

A South African soldier wounded during operations in Namibia against SWAPO is helped onto a waiting helicopter.

'The ultimate aim of the Soviet Union and its allies was to overthrow the present body politic [government] in the Republic of South Africa and to replace it with a Marxist-orientated form of government to further the objectives of the USSR. Therefore all possible methods and means are used to attain this objective. This includes instigating social and labour unrest, civilian resistance, terrorist attacks against . . . South Africa, and the intimidation of black leaders and members of the security forces. This onslaught is supported by a worldwide propaganda campaign and the involvement of various front organizations, such as trade unions and even certain church organizations and leaders.' South African Prime Minister P W Botha outlining the justification for total strategy, 1978.

end there and the armed forces were to appear frequently in Angola on the pretence of searching out Namibian SWAPO guerrillas. Later, raids into Angola were designed to assist the opposition forces of the Angolan UNITA group, led by Jonas Savimbi. By supporting UNITA, the South African government hoped to break the rule of the Marxist MPLA government. Eventually, however, both sides (MPLA and UNITA) reached a stalemate position and South Africa was forced to agree to a UN resolution demanding the withdrawal of South African forces from Namibia. This led to Namibian independence in March 1990 which meant that South Africa could no longer base troops in Namibia or directly threaten the Angolan border.

For landlocked Botswana, there has never been much opportunity to resist 'total strategy'. After independence (1966), Botswana attempted to join with other newly independent African states and oppose apartheid. However, the South African government could disrupt Botswana's economy at will because it relied so heavily on South Africa. For example, refrigerated trucks would be unavailable just at the time Botswana needed to export its meat, or oil supplies would dry up just as the Christmas travel period arrived, or if oil was bought from elsewhere, the storage tanks would be destroyed (as was also the case in Angola).

In addition, Botswana has difficult relations with other Southern African states. Botswana produces 30 per cent of all the diamonds mined around the world which gives the country a degree of economic security and wealth which many other countries do not enjoy. Also, its geographical location has made Botswana a haven for people from both Zimbabwe and

South Africa who seek refuge – one reason why relations between those countries and Botswana have never been very good.

Lesotho is in a similar situation to Botswana but far poorer, as is Swaziland – the third so-called 'captive state'. In Lesotho, South Africa has supported the rebel Lesotho Liberation Army which has frequently mounted attacks against the country's essential services. The policy of destabilization has been so successful that in 1986 it brought the downfall of the government in a military coup. Swaziland has also been caught in the middle, with apartheid South Africa on the one side and Marxist Mozambique on the other. With rare exceptions, the policy of the government of Swaziland has been to do whatever the South African government demands.

In direct contrast, Swaziland's other neighbour, Mozambique, has been severely affected by the destabilization strategy. Here South Africa has attempted to weaken the economy, wreck the

Damage to a suspected ANC base in Botswana; it was attacked by South African troops.

transport system and force the government not to allow the ANC to use Mozambique as a refuge. Because Mozambique has so few natural resources it relies upon revenue for transporting raw materials from landlocked countries to the port of Beira.

First Ian Smith's Rhodesian government and then the South African government have used Renamo, also known as the MNR, a resistance group opposed to the ruling Frelimo government of Mozambique. By 1984 Renamo's actions had forced the Marxist President Machel to negotiate with South Africa. In the Nkomati Accord Mozambique agreed to stop supporting the ANC and South Africa agreed to cease support for Renamo. The deal had little long-term effect on either country, although Mozambique did, at first, expel ANC members from the country. In the early 1990s Mozambique was effectively split between Renamo (holding the countryside) and Frelimo (holding the cities with troop support from Zimbabwe), although there were moves towards peace talks.

Between Rhodesia's declaration of UDI and independence in 1979, Ian Smith's government became increasingly dependent upon South Africa for military and economic support. South Africa was keen to see the failure of international attempts to impose economic sanctions against Rhodesia, because success might encourage attempts to do the same against South Africa.

After independence, the new Zimbabwean government was in favour of policies based upon a multiracial society. However, although

> **The costs and casualties of the civil war in Mozambique.**
> 'By 1988 Renamo had forced 870,000 Mozambicans to flee as refugees, 1 million villagers inside the country had been displaced and 2.5 million were at risk from starvation. About 100,000 civilians had been killed and a far greater number maimed or wounded. In 1988 a famine threatened 6 million people. In 1989 it was estimated that 7.7 million people, almost half the country's total population, needed food aid to survive.' Guy Arnold, *Wars in the Third World Since 1945.*

Oil tanks in Angola destroyed by South African forces. Such attacks are intended to weaken, or destabilize, the Angolan government. Angola's economy relies on income from the oil industry.

Zimbabwe was economically strong and becoming more so, fifteen years of isolation had increased its dependence upon South Africa. This made Zimbabwean politicians unwilling to move too fast against South Africa.

Meanwhile South African forces bombed suspected ANC bases in Zimbabwe, virtually at will. And by also continuing guerilla activity in Mozambique, Zimbabwean forces were kept fully occupied guarding and repairing road and rail links through Mozambique to ports on the east coast.

Zambia has suffered from the destabilization campaign on account of its considerable active support for the region's liberation movements. During the UDI period in Rhodesia (1965-79), South African troops were stationed on the Zambian border and on several occasions South African troops have attacked Zambia from their Namibian bases. South African-backed UNITA rebels from Angola have also made attacks, and there have been direct attacks on ANC bases.

In Malawi, President Banda's controversial policy to establish friendly relations with South Africa has saved the country from the worst aspects of destabilization which can be seen elsewhere. However, even this controversial policy did not save Malawi from suffering from the total strategy policy. Malawi's shortest route to the sea is the direct railway line from Blantyre to the Mozambique port of Nacala, some 600km. Renamo have ensured that this route has been inactive for many years, so Malawi has been forced to export its goods from Durban, in South Africa, which means that exports are less profitable for Malawi and imports more expensive.

The so-called 'low intensity' conflict mounted by the South African government, its intelligence forces, the armed forces and its allies, such as UNITA and Renamo, are at the centre of Southern Africa's most deep-seated tragedy. The constant experience of war conditions has seriously disrupted development and demoralized the black population. There are however, signs of positive change on the horizon.

REFORM IN SOUTH AFRICA

The shooting of hundreds of black schoolchildren in Soweto in 1976 was the start of a new, increasingly violent phase in South African conflict, which continued on into the 1980s. On 20 August 1983 at a huge rally near Cape Town, the United Democratic Front (UDF) was formed. Unlike previous groups, it was not a single political party, but an 'umbrella' organization helping to co-ordinate the activities of nearly 600 different anti-apartheid organizations. Another new focus for black protest was created in 1985, in the form of the Confederation of South African Trade Unions (COSATU), made up of thirty-four unions. COSATU demanded the release of Nelson Mandela (Vice-President of the ANC) and the abolition of the pass laws, and urged countries to withdraw investment from South Africa in order to destabilize the white government.

Violent conflict was a regular feature of life in the townships in South Africa throughout the 1980s and into the 1990s. This photograph shows a victim of a riot in 1991.

Reform?

In response to a growing tide of pressure from inside South Africa and from foreign countries, in 1984 the government attempted a series of changes to the constitution to draw in Asians and coloureds, but maintain the exclusion of blacks. A new constitution was adopted by the (whites-only) House of Assembly on 25 January 1985. It set up three houses of parliament: the House of Representatives for coloureds; the House of Delegates for Asians and the House of Assembly for whites. Most Asians and coloured people rejected the new constitution because it left out black people. In the first elections to the new houses of parliament, only 14 per cent of the Asian and coloured electorate voted. In reality, little had changed.

Black Africans protested against the new constitution. The occupants of the black townships were deeply frustrated and, for many, things could hardly get worse. Thereafter opposition to the government increased in a variety of ways. For example, in 1985, the Vaal townships' residents started a rent strike, and throughout the country blacks boycotted

A mother holds up her new-born baby in a house in Alexandra Township, Johannesburg, 1987. Such a house, with no running water, no electricity and hardly any space, was typical of conditions in the townships – areas next to big cities where blacks were allowed to live.

white-run shops and businesses. Increasingly, demonstrations would start spontaneously and, often because of police actions, turn into riots.

There were also increasing numbers of reprisals against blacks who collaborated with the armed forces or who acted as informers. One notorious treatment of collaborators was the 'necklace', which involved forcing a car tyre soaked in petrol over the victim and setting light to it.

In an attempt to control the situation, the government imposed a state of emergency in some areas of the country in July 1985, which was lifted less than a year later, but then reimposed almost immediately in June 1986 across the whole of South Africa with a series of even harsher measures. Some 30,000 people were detained, virtually all opposition groups were banned and several townships were occupied by the armed forces. Meanwhile, the policy of forced

removals of people (mostly Asian and Coloured) in accordance with the Group Areas Act continued. In 1983-84 almost 130,000 Coloured and Asian families were removed to new areas. Also, black families continued to be moved out into the homelands. In 1986 some 60,000 blacks were moved into homelands, a policy which entailed tearing down the homes of 2,425 'squatter' families.

Resistance from the black population was considerable and included the use of armed force, mass protests, national strikes, the collapse of local government and the education system. Clearly, the ANC was intent on not just revolt but revolution as well.

End to apartheid?
In 1986 the government announced that it would dismantle apartheid. However, for years the

'This [the June 1986 State of Emergency] provided a cover for a reign of state terror, involving detentions, murders by clandestine 'hit squads' and vigilante groups, the insertion of the SADF [South African Defence Force] into the administration of townships – through so-called mini-Joint Management Committees – and the imposition of press censorship, which is largely responsible for the disappearance of pictures of unrest from the world's television screens.' (Rob Davies et al, *The Struggle for South Africa: A Reference Guide to Movements, Organizations and Institutions*.)

government had been claiming 'apartheid is dead' and the reforms did not make a fundamental change. For instance the hated pass laws were abolished in 1986, but a policy of 'orderly urbanization' was introduced instead, which meant the authorities still closely controlled the movement of black people.

In the second half of 1986, reform was slowed and the government concentrated on a campaign of repression against anyone opposed to it. But the government increasingly found itself unable to keep order. On 2 February 1990 the South African President, F W de Klerk, announced a series of sweeping changes, including the legalization of the ANC and the release of Nelson Mandela after twenty-seven years in jail. De Klerk also announced that the death penalty would be reviewed and, for the time being, suspended.

The change of heart of the white government was due both to changes in the international system and within South Africa. Within the government itself there were important changes in the balance of power following the resignation of de Klerk's predecessor, P W Botha. Botha was forced to resign after proving unable to find

Johannesburg, March 1986: Police use rhino whips to disperse protesting students. South African police have often been accused of using excessive force in their attempts to keep order.

solutions to the disorder which swept the country in 1989.

The removal of Botha opened the way for F W de Klerk, a politician less keen on relying on security forces and willing to try to find a political solution. In order to implement change, de Klerk succeeded in dismantling the National Security Management System, a nationwide structure designed to preserve and further the aims of apartheid. By cutting down the size of the security forces the government released money for welfare programmes to assist those most affected by poverty.

However, one of the most positive steps was the start of talks between the government, the ANC and other representatives of black, Coloured and Asian people. The talks (formally called the Convention for a Democratic South Africa, or Codesa) started in December 1991. The aim was to lay a basis for democracy, setting up a multi-racial government which would be in control of South Africa during elections (in which all South Africans over eighteen would get a vote). Yet there remained big differences of opinion between the two sides and negotiations moved very slowly. The potential for violence remained high, both between the ANC and other black organizations, particularly Inkatha (see below), and from the white conservatives.

Crucial to the success of negotiations was the need for both sides to recognize the pressures on each. De Klerk contended with some extreme conservative forces, such as the Afrikaner Resistance Movement (AWB). Nelson Mandela had to try to hold together different elements of the anti-apartheid movement such as the South African Communist Party and the trade unions. The Codesa talks were aided by a referendum on 19 March 1992 in which all white South Africans were asked whether they supported democratic reform. Over 68 per cent of whites said 'yes'.

Inkatha and the ANC

Above all the ANC will have to arrive at a settlement with the Inkatha movement, led by Chief Gatsha Buthelezi. The ANC and its allies largely aim to express the hopes of all the varied

Chief Gatsha Buthelezi, Zulu leader of the Inkatha movement. Inkatha is one of the rivals to the ANC for support of black South Africans. Zulus make up just over a fifth of the black population.

black groups in South Africa. However, Inkatha is derived from the Zulu tribe and, by opposing the ANC, Inkatha hopes to emerge as a key black organization. Inkatha leaders looked to influence the Codesa talks and so command a more powerful position in the future. But the fact that Inkatha does not represent anything like the majority of the black population, or even the majority of Zulus, has caused tension and considerable bloodshed between black factions and is possibly an obstacle to a peaceful transition to democracy. Between August 1990 and January 1991, conflict between Inkatha and the ANC led to the loss of 1,000 lives in Johannesburg and, since mid-1987, 3,000 deaths in Natal. Indeed, Chief Buthelezi has recognized that Inkatha's potential for disruption is his main weapon. He appears to be using this as a means to command a political position of greater importance than his national support might justify. Some opinion polls have rated his support among all blacks at 3 per cent, while his support among Zulus may be as low as 10 per cent.

THE HUMAN COST OF CONFLICT

It is to be hoped that the new spirit of compromise in South Africa will see a genuine end both to apartheid and to the policy of 'total strategy' which has been used to defend it. Even so, the impact upon the region has been devastating and the human cost enormous – problems will continue for many years. The children of the region have been hit particularly hard.

When Southern African states became independent they were extremely poor because of their colonial past. Basically, European states acquired colonies because they offered access to the raw materials, land and agricultural products which were not available in Europe. The desire to bring civilization and Christianity to so-called 'backward' areas was much less prominent than is often thought. Besides, it is arguable as to how much these peoples needed the help of outsiders. There is a good deal of evidence which points to the existence of rich and diverse African cultures before the arrival of the Europeans.

Colonial powers took far more out of their colonies than they were prepared to put back in. Consequently, when African states acquired independence, their countries had a great deal of agriculture and mining, but little industry. Also, poor standards of education made it difficult to find the numbers of people needed to run the

A typical school for blacks in South Africa, in the Transkei homeland. Despite being the wealthiest country in Southern Africa, South Africa provides poor facilities for black schoolchildren.

The civil war in Angola has left thousands of civilians and soldiers dead and many more wounded.

through agricultural produce and mining, it was not long before the supply of certain foods and minerals exceeded demand. Prices dropped, and governments found themselves deeply in debt to the banks in richer countries. Western banks made big loans to developing countries in the 1960s and 1970s, but when the projects funded with the money stopped being profitable, the loans proved to be a heavy burden.

Developing countries found themselves having to produce more to achieve the same amount of income. Income earned in currencies such as American dollars or German marks (currencies which are not likely to lose too much value too quickly) must usually be used to pay for imports. A shortage of foreign currency can be very serious when tractors, fertilizers and medicines are required. Because many of these imports may take the form of weapons as well, a part of South Africa's destabilization programme concentrated upon the destruction of enterprises such as tea estates and cement plants which earn foreign currency. Without foreign currency, countries simply cannot trade. Many countries have built up huge debts to international banks and now find it more and more difficult to find loans for development.

Successful development projects have become war targets. A new school or health clinic is an easy, undefended target. Since 1982 over 800 health posts and centres have either been destroyed or closed in Mozambique. There is also widespread evidence of rebel groups being responsible for theft, rape, arson, crop destruction, mass murder, enforced conscription and enslavement of labour.

Throughout Southern Africa approximately twenty-five children die each hour from the direct and indirect effects of war. In Mozambique alone 100,000 civilians were killed in 1986 and 1987 and a high proportion were children. Between 1980 and 1992, some 1.3 million people have died as a result of conflict in Angola and Mozambique and 11 million people have been driven from their homes at least once.

Mozambique and Angola have been forced to bear the brunt of the human cost of conflict in

economies and the civil services. In Mozambique, for example, when the Portuguese left, 70 per cent of the population had no access to health care of any type and 93 per cent of the population was illiterate. The situation in Angola was much the same. More recently, the tactics of the South African government in supporting rebel guerrilla forces in the front-line states made the task of development in those states twice as difficult.

Those countries dependent upon the export of raw materials and agricultural products were extremely vulnerable. With so-called 'Third World' countries trying to develop rapidly

CHAPTER 7

Southern Africa. However, other countries have also suffered. Most governments have been compelled to spend more than they can ever afford to defend themselves against South Africa and guerrilla forces supported by South Africa. With so much spent on defence, less is available for development. Although Malawi is one of the most densely populated African countries it has been forced to accept over 600,000 refugees from neighbouring Mozambique. Whereas the country once produced enough food to feed its population, this is no longer the case.

Although many Southern African states have placed great stress upon education for all, successes have been reversed in many areas. In 1986 two-thirds of the children in Angola received a full education, but by 1992 the figure was less than half. If people are literate they can make better use of the information available, particularly information about health care. Studies have shown that where there is a greater level of literacy there tends to be better child care and fewer infant deaths.

Children – the first to suffer

One of the saddest aspects of the conflict is the effect upon children. In Mozambique up to half a million children have been orphaned, abandoned or injured during the continuing guerrilla warfare. Apart from seeing their homes destroyed, many have been forced out of their villages and towns. Thousands of these children have seen relatives and friends killed and mutilated, often for the smallest of reasons. Rebel groups have press-ganged young children and forced them into training camps – which has meant that they are fighting and killing by the time they are just thirteen or fourteen.

Thousands of civilians throughout Southern Africa have been injured in guerrilla warfare. Many of them are permanently disabled. Even now this continues because of the thousands of land mines which have been laid. Many civilians lose their lives or limbs when unexploded mines are set off by herdsmen and farmers.

Within South Africa itself, people may suffer less from the effects of violence, although this

This clinic at Marrambula in Mozambique was partially destroyed by Renamo guerrillas but continued to function.

An Angolan clinic specializing in helping people injured in the civil war. Laurinda Chinginila (centre) learns to walk again after losing both legs when she stepped on a UNITA land mine.

'My name is Patricio Nthupuela. I am from Zambezi [in Mozambique]. I came to Maputo to try and find a prosthesis [artificial limb] for my maimed arm. Early in 1983 I decided to continue with my studies at a district located 100 kilometres from Marrun, my motherland. There were no good living conditions in Marrun because of what armed bandits did. One day the car I was travelling in blew up due to a land mine laid by the bandits. In the explosion I lost both my arms . . . I learned to write using my mouth. I passed the 4th and 5th degrees and now I am attending 6 . . . I have tried very hard to get a prosthesis but unfortunately I never had a chance. The bandits killed my parents and other people and they created a lot of destruction. On 19 December 1986 they kidnapped my sister and my nephews. Only I managed to escape. Now I have no relatives.' *Children On The Front-line - A Report for UNICEF.*

itself is bad enough, especially in clashes between police and demonstrators. However, despite the fact that South Africa is a relatively wealthy country, apartheid has meant that most black people do not benefit from it. For example, a very high proportion of deaths among black children are due to diarrhoea, tuberculosis and measles, all of which can be easily prevented and cured with inexpensive health care. In the case of diarrhoea, children usually die from dehydration, even though this can be easily combated by a simple process which involves administering a mix of salt and sugar dissolved in clean water. Yet, these basic medicines are often out of reach for poor black families.

The list of examples of how people have suffered as a result of conflict in Southern Africa is almost endless. In effect it is a vicious circle in which conflict slows down development which in turn creates more conflict.

FOOD IN SOUTHERN AFRICA

I n most cases, countries in Southern Africa are able to produce enough food to feed everyone. Yet, many people cannot buy the food produced, either because it costs too much, or because the storehouses in the cities are badly used. With roads in poor condition, and railways sabotaged by rebel guerrillas, at times it can be very difficult to get food out to the countryside. In some areas there is actually a shortage of food because farmers have been forced to leave their land to get away from fighting between rebels and government forces.

The areas worst hit by food shortages are Angola and Mozambique, although Malawi is also badly affected. Serious food shortages and virtual famines have been both caused and made worse by the guerrilla warfare. Food shortages affect both the countryside and the cities. In the countryside, farmers who once lived off what they grew often become homeless – losing their only source of food and income. Serious droughts in 1988 and 1989 affected all countries except Botswana and Zimbabwe. Although relief operations have been mounted, communities in remote areas sometimes receive aid too late – especially if bridges, roads and railway lines have been destroyed.

In the cities, with extremely low wages and fierce competition for jobs, people are left with hardly enough money to buy food. So it is possible to be both employed and hungry. It is much easier for relief programmes to reach people in cities, but their numbers are rising rapidly and it

In 1990 Angola suffered appalling drought and famine – the shortage of food was made worse by the continuing civil war.

South African farms are very productive – but many black South Africans cannot afford to buy enough of the food produced.

'Reaching the outlying areas is very difficult. The roads have been cut, which means we can't transport produce. Very often, we manage to buy and store produce only to find that the *"bandidos"* [Renamo guerrillas] then burn it. AGRICOM is a target because we are responsible for marketing food in the rural areas. Our transport fleet has suffered great damage. About thirty vehicles have been destroyed, and we are left with only nine. Even in the accessible areas, drought has reduced production.' Ricardo Joao, 1987 local director of AGRICOM, state-run agricultural production and marketing agency in Mozambique.

has proved difficult to keep pace. Refugees tend to be drawn into cities and towns because they know the chance of finding food is much higher.

It is not easy to grow crops in the harsh Namibian climate. In recent years, while large amounts of food have had to be imported from South Africa, equally large amounts of beef, mutton and wool were exported by South African farmers in Namibia. So most Namibians have to buy imported food, often on the poor wages sent back by Namibians working in South Africa. Meanwhile the amount of food crops grown has remained very low.

Namibia has also seen its rich fishing grounds plundered by South African, Russian and Spanish fishing fleets. Although scientists warned that fish stocks would diminish if fishing carried on at such a high level, the foreign fleets took no notice. By 1980, catches had fallen to one-seventh their level in 1968.

For so long as conflict continues in Southern Africa there will be problems of food shortages and hunger. Refugees are invariably reluctant to return to their homes for the very reasons which forced them to leave – attacks from guerrillas, drought, small crop yields and environmental damage, such as soil erosion. In Southern Africa there may be food shortages for some time to come, especially in Namibia, Angola and Mozambique.

Without peace and stability, aid will continually fail to arrive at the places it is most needed. Cattle will be in too short supply to aid ploughing. Seeds will not be distributed and farmers will not have the money to buy them. Refugees will not return to their homes, farms will become run down and towns and cities will remain overcrowded. Those who are in absolute poverty will probably die. Those who are vulnerable will sink into absolute poverty. Nor will aid organizations like Oxfam and Save the Children be able to help indefinitely – already they complain that relief has overtaken efforts to

'We now have upwards of 12,000 displaced people who are getting no other assistance from any official or unofficial source apart from what they can get from the local villagers who are good enough to receive them even though they are needy themselves . . . In Mozambique, they have been robbed of their maize and livestock. Sometimes their clothes have been taken, and their villages burned. Many have had relatives murdered. Many have been separated from their families and it is not known if they are alive or dead. I have met groups of children of about 12 years old, travelling together with no one to look after them.' Oxfam report on situation in Dezda, along the Mozambique/ Malawi border, March 1986.

Victims of war, 1985. Mozambican refugees in the South African homeland of Gazankulu, near the Mozambique border. Having fled from both Renamo and Frelimo, they end up in a country where they are unwanted.

20 April, 1990: a truck carrying food aid to a rural area of Mozambique. The photographer reported that as the truck passed the government soldiers (left) they threatened to shoot the tyres and take the food. On this occasion they did not shoot and the food got through.

encourage development, which means that the local people will be less and less able to help themselves.

Children are the most vulnerable to food

The daily diet of a three-and-a-half-year-old black child from Stellenbosch, South Africa:
Breakfast: Slice of brown bread and margarine; coffee with half teaspoon of sugar and Cremora [condensed milk];
Lunch: Coffee with half teaspoon of sugar and Cremora;
Supper: Coffee with half teaspoon of sugar and Cremora;
Between Meals: Dry bread.
The Zulu diet of the past included meat for periodic feasts, quantities of amasi (sour milk), and a wide range of vegetables including sorghum, millet, pumpkins, gourds, melons, yams, various tubers similar to the potato, various nuts and indigenous beans and a wide variety of green beans and plants.

Source: *Children on the Front Line: A Report for UNICEF*, 1989.

shortages. Over half of the children in Mozambique suffer malnutrition of one form or another and stunted growth is widespread. There is also extensive malnutrition amongst mothers, which prevents breastfeeding, the most effective way of giving a child natural immunity to disease. In South Africa there is also widespread evidence of malnutrition amongst the black population. About 31 per cent of pre-school children who live in the countryside are underweight.

South Africa, unlike other countries in the region, is far from poor. If the total wealth of the country is divided by the number of people, the amount of money per person is seven times higher than in China or Sri Lanka. Without doubt South Africa is a wealthy enough country to feed all its population. However, thousands of black, coloured and Asian people in South Africa are so poor that they do not get enough to eat. It is to be hoped that, if the apartheid system goes for good, hunger and poor·health will be less of a feature of life for most South Africans.

CHAPTER 9

THE EFFECT ON THE ENVIRONMENT

One of the major problems facing poor and underdeveloped countries is the growing threat to the environment. If societies cannot or are unable to find a balance between what they take from the environment and what they give back, eventually there will be nothing left to take. If forests are cut down too quickly it will take centuries for them to be replenished and the soil beneath will be quickly eroded by wind and rain. If fields are cultivated too intensively the goodness in the land will eventually disappear. If some parts of the natural world are destroyed, there are always others that are affected.

Ivory trade
The wildlife in Southern Africa has suffered from human conflict. Parts of Angola are virtually devoid of wildlife. Angola's rebel forces, UNITA, have paid for their arms by illegally exporting ivory (from elephant tusks and rhino horns). In September 1989 a shipment of almost 1,000 tusks was intercepted leaving UNITA territory. For similar reasons the elephant population in Mozambique declined from 55,000 in 1979 to 17,000 in 1987 to less than 10,000 in 1992. Rhinoceroses are also hunted for the same reasons. Throughout Africa the rhinoceros population has fallen from 60,000 in 1970 to a total of no more than 3,500 in 1992.

A shipment of twelve tonnes of elephant tusks is destroyed after being captured in Kenya, 1989. In desperate times, smuggling elephant and rhino tusks is one way to make money.

South Africa is well known for its lush farmland and good weather, and the country does not suffer from over-population. Nevertheless, parts of South Africa do contain areas where the environment has been severely damaged.

The policy of the white government of creating black homelands (from 1961 onwards) is a clear example of apartheid's damaging effect upon the environment. In these areas the quality of land is very poor and there is only about half the amount of land needed to feed the people living there. Most of the land is only good enough for raising livestock. As people attempt to gain more and more from a small area of land, pastures become overgrazed. With the grass cover removed, the topsoil is left bare and can easily be eroded by wind and rain. In some homelands, such as Ciskei, almost one half of the land has been severely damaged.

The same is also true of South Africa's forests

40

In some of the homelands of South Africa, as here in the Transkei, the land is badly overgrazed, which leads to soil erosion.

where two-thirds of the population rely upon wood for fuel and each person uses up to 800 kg per year. Several of the poorer parts of South Africa are in a deficit position – where a growing population uses more wood than the forests can produce – and the forests may eventually be destroyed. Around one half of the black population are forced to live in the homelands. The rest of the black population lives in segregated townships and squatter settlements. For so long as these people remain poor and forced by law to live in overcrowded areas in which the land cannot provide sufficient food, the environment will suffer badly.

South Africa has extensive mineral resources. It has some of the world's biggest deposits of gold, diamonds, chromite and platinum and substantial amounts of coal, silver and iron ore. These minerals have secured a reliable source of money for the government. But in order to gain

as much as possible in the least time, the government has not imposed strict regulations concerning the environment or safety. Mining, if not treated with care, can be very damaging to the environment. Blasting, digging and the movement of vast quantities of material for grinding and crushing can dramatically alter landscapes. The chemicals needed to treat the ores or the smelting process may lead to a number of harmful residues, such as sulphur dioxide and lead which cause serious pollution.

In South Africa many areas have been strip mined, which is the most environmentally harmful way of extracting ore, and one of the main ways in which water supplies become polluted. For example, the Mngweni River, which flows through the Kwazulu reserve has been known to contain mercury deposits 1,500 times greater than levels permitted in the USA.

Without expensive safety procedures the

Women in Gazankulu, South Africa, gather firewood. Throughout most of Southern Africa, wood is the only available fuel for cooking and heating. As a result, many forests have been destroyed.

human cost to the mineworkers can be high. For every tonne of gold South Africa extracts, a black miner dies in an accident. In all, by the end of 1991, 46,000 South African miners had died this century from underground accidents.

Many of the world's oil exporters from the Middle East and Africa refuse to sell to South Africa, even though the only formal ban on trade concerns defence equipment. Consequently, South Africa has become heavily dependent upon its abundant coal resources. In areas where coal-fired power stations are in use, air pollution is very high because the waste gases are not cleaned before entering the atmosphere.

Elsewhere in Southern Africa the combination of persistent conflict and war on the one hand and extreme economic underdevelopment on the other have combined to create several environmental dangers. In Lesotho, 10 per cent of the original farmland is barren waste and 90 per cent of grazing and cropland is being over-farmed or overgrazed.

Warfare of all kinds can damage the environment. Bombs and shells, military vehicles driving cross-country and large numbers of marching troops can all cause large-scale harm. In general, the less fierce the level of conflict the fewer are the environmental problems which occur. However, although the armed conflicts in Southern Africa have usually been low-level,

'Small-scale peasant agriculture was also seriously affected by the war . . . [One] reason was that the standing crops of those who stayed were frequently destroyed by the army as [South African] armoured trucks were driven across crops, and often through homelands [in Namibia].' Susanna Smith, *Front Line Africa: The Right to a Future.*

there are environmental costs. In Angola and Mozambique, rebel forces have at times been too weak to confront government forces. Instead they have adopted tactics designed to demoralize the local people by harming their environment. Fields and roads have been mined to prevent food from reaching the cities. Agricultural centres have become military targets. As refugees flood into the cities of Malawi and Zimbabwe the areas for kilometres around are picked over for firewood – leading to yet more environmental damage.

Tropical hardwoods (like mahogany or teak), as well as ivory, have been exploited to pay for war costs. Satellite images have shown marked deforestation in UNITA-controlled areas of Angola. With the exception of Zimbabwe, the majority of the front-line states have seen their economies and environments decline because of South Africa's policy of destabilization. As land is lost to erosion, it becomes increasingly difficult to produce enough food – and the pressure on the remaining good land is such that it too may well be eroded in a few years. Without an end to conflict, and a co-ordinated programme of aid to farmers, the problem is likely to get worse.

Many parts of Southern Africa, such as the area of southern Namibia pictured here, have a harsh and arid environment. The dividing line between ecological balance and environmental disaster is very fine.

CHAPTER 10

THE FUTURE OF SOUTHERN AFRICA

By far the most important changes have been those in South Africa, where there is now real hope that apartheid will finally give way to democracy with the imposition of a multi-party system. This will mean that, in theory, blacks will live in equality with whites. However, given the big difference between rich and poor, white and black, there is a long way to go.

The end of the Cold War between the USA and the Soviet Union, and then the breakup of the Soviet Union in 1991, have helped the chances of peace in Southern Africa. After the Second World War, the Soviet Union gave military or financial support to the Marxist independence movements. For instance, the Cuban troops sent to Angola to aid the MPLA in 1975 were supplied with Soviet equipment. Opposing the MPLA, UNITA received financial support from the USA. Successive South African governments have stressed the threat of communism in the region (to attempt to get US support) while other Southern African states have appealed to communist countries, such as the Soviet Union and Cuba, for help in countering 'total strategy'.

April, 1990: a starving child in Mugulama, Mozambique, is weighed by a relief worker. Mugulama had just been recaptured by the government from Renamo guerrillas.

However, as relations between the superpowers improved, they withdrew the type of support which increased conflict in the region. With the collapse of the Soviet Union, and deepening recession in the USA, there was no longer a superpower with the will or resources to supply large amounts of arms and money to any government or rebels in Southern Africa.

Political changes within South Africa may also help to bring an end to conflict in neighbouring countries. The removal of South African forces from Namibia, and Namibian independence (in 1989) have made way for another peace process, this time in Angola. One reason for continued conflict in Angola is that UNITA does command a degree of political support in certain parts of the country. And while US support for UNITA has been reduced, the supply of military equipment to the MPLA from the former Soviet Union has ceased altogether.

On 31 May 1991 the Angolan government (MPLA) and UNITA signed a peace agreement –

7 March 1992, Johannesburg, South Africa: demonstrating members of the right-wing AWB organization (on horseback) break through a police blockade. Right-wing whites are likely to oppose any government elected by a majority of South Africans.

the Estoril Accord. This agreement set out that multi-party elections should take place in 1992 and the MPLA and UNITA military forces be merged into a national army. Angola has great economic potential but it is still likely that conflict there will continue. There are some people within South Africa and the USA who may not wish to see the peace process succeed, in the hope that UNITA will achieve a military victory. In 1992 the Angolan economy was extremely weak and economic reforms were planned which would mean that the situation would get worse before getting better.

Elsewhere throughout the region, there are some indications of a better future. Talks are in progress in Mozambique in an attempt to bring the civil war to an end. In Zambia President Kaunda has recently been voted out of power which proves that democracy is alive and well. Zimbabwe has shown how much can be achieved after only a decade or so of independence, especially in the agricultural sector. The country's 'Growth with Equity' development programme has been broadly successful. Although there were some lean years in between, the Zimbabwean economy grew by 10.7 per cent in 1980 and 5.3 per cent in 1988. There has also been a welcome improvement in health care which has led to less infant deaths. In the late-1970s, before independence, up to 220 babies per thousand died before reaching their first birthday. The figure dropped to 72 by the end of 1987.

However, most people in Southern Africa are now worse off than thirty years ago. The environment has been damaged, people have been worn down by years of conflict and there is little trust in the future. These are the major factors which must be confronted if conflict in the region is to be erased on a permanent rather than a temporary basis.

GLOSSARY

Afrikaans The language of the Afrikaners. It is similar to the Dutch and Flemish spoken by the first Dutch settlers in Southern Africa. It is the official language of the Republic of South Africa.

Afrikaners *See Boers.*

ANC (African National Congress) One of the major black anti-apartheid groups, previously banned in South Africa.

Apartheid An Afrikaans word, meaning apartness. It has come to be used to describe racial segregation and hence the system of government in South Africa based upon total supremacy of the white, minority population.

AWB (Afrikanerweerstandsbeweging, or Afrikaner Resistance Movement) Right-wing movement of white South Africans who support apartheid and oppose moves to give the vote to all South Africans.

Boers Dutch settlers in South Africa; from around 1910 they came to be known as Afrikaners.

Colonialism Control and rule of regions now known as the South, or Third World, by major European powers, especially in the nineteenth century.

Commonwealth An international organization which comprises Britain, its dominions, such as Australia and Canada, and most of its former colonies.

Constitution A charter, or set of rules, to control the actions of a government.

COSATU (Confederation of South African Trade Unions) The central organization for the biggest non-white trade unions in South Africa; formed in 1984.

Coup An attempt to overthrow the existing government with a sudden, surprise action.

Developing country One of the world's poorer countries. Compared to countries like the USA and those of Western Europe, all the countries in Africa are poor, and are classed as developing countries. The term can be misleading because poorer countries are often 'developing' slower than richer, 'developed' countries.

Economic sanctions Actions taken by one or more countries against another, to punish or control it, by stopping some or all goods from being sold to it or bought from it.

FNLA (Frente Nacional de Libertação de Angola) A political/military group opposed to the MPLA government of Angola. The FNLA has been based in Zaire. Its main support comes from the Bakongo people.

Frelimo (Frente de Libertação de Moçambique) The Marxist governing party in Mozambique since 1975.

Front-line states Countries that formed a collective front against South Africa and backed the armed struggle against the white regime led by Ian Smith in Rhodesia and the white government in South Africa. They were: Tanzania, Zambia, Angola, Mozambique. Later additions were: Zimbabwe (1980) and Namibia (1989).

Indigenous people The first people to live in an area or country.

Land mine An explosive device placed in the ground, usually detonated by stepping or driving on it.

Landlocked Completely surrounded by land. A landlocked country is one which has no access to the sea.

Marxist Follower of the economic and political theory that class struggle is the way to achieve change, and that capitalism will ultimately be replaced by communism.

MNR (Movimento Nacionale de Resistência de Moçambique) Another name for Renamo (see below).

MPLA (Movimento Popular de Libertação de Angola) The Marxist organization which has largely controlled Angola since the civil war which followed independence in 1975.

Multi-party system Democracy which allows any number of political parties to contest elections.

Non-Aligned Movement The group of Third World countries which attempted to remain outside the influence of the superpowers during the Cold War.

PAC (Pan-Africanist Congress) The South African organization established by members of the ANC who stressed the importance of solidarity amongst black Africans, and were suspicious of sympathetic coloured, Asian or white groups.

Pass laws Laws which required black people in South Africa to carry identification.

Raw materials Products which form the basis of industrial manufacture – oil, iron ore, etc.

Renamo (Resistência Nacionale Moçambicana) The political/military group in Mozambique opposed to the Marxist Frelimo government.

SASO (South African Students Organization) Formed in 1975, SASO was a focus for the Black Consciousness movement.

Segregation The act of keeping apart people from different races or groups.

Strip mining Mining by digging from the surface over a large area (as opposed to digging a narrow shaft down to the ore).

Suez Canal The canal built (1854-69) to create an opening between the Mediterranean Sea and the Red Sea, to enable shipping to avoid the long and dangerous journey around Africa, especially the Cape of Good Hope.

SWAPO (South West Africa People's Organization) The Namibian freedom fighters who, in 1990, formed the country's first independent government.

Third World The term used to describe the developing countries of Africa, Asia and Latin America.

UDF (United Democratic Front) The South

African umbrella organization for anti-apartheid groups, formed in 1983 while many of the key anti-apartheid organizations (such as the ANC and PAC) were banned.

UNITA (União Nacional para a Independência Total de Angola)   The Angolan political/military organization opposed to the Marxist MPLA (see above).

UN (United Nations)   The organization formed in 1945 with the aim of maintaining international peace. All nations have the right to membership. Delegations from all member countries sit on the General Assembly, and fifteen countries are members of the Security Council. The USA, Russia, Britain, France and China all have permanent seats on the Security Council.

FURTHER INFORMATION

There are a number of organizations concerned with events in Southern Africa which have resource bases and sometimes publish books and newsletters. Some such organizations are: the Anti-Apartheid Movement, the Defence and Aid Fund for Southern Africa, Oxfam and the Catholic Institute for International Relations. For recent information about the countries in Southern Africa, try contacting the information office of their embassy. Or you could refer to an almanac such as the Encyclopedia Britannica *Book of the Year*.

Newspapers
All the main newspapers carry reports of major events in Southern Africa. If you want to track down contemporary news reports of an event some years ago, go to your local reference library, where newspapers are usually held on microfilm.

General reading
Baynham, Dr Simon *Africa from 1945* (Franklin Watts, 1987)
Harris, Sarah *Sharpeville* (Dryad Press, 1988)
Hayward, Jean *South Africa since 1948* (Wayland, 1989)
Omond, Roger *Steve Biko and apartheid* (Evans Brothers, 1991)
Tames, Richard *Nelson Mandela* (Franklin Watts, 1991)

Some more advanced general books:
Hanlon, J *Beggar Your Neighbours: Apartheid Power in Southern Africa* (Catholic Institute for International Relations, 1986)
Huddlestone, Trevor *Return to South Africa: The Ecstasy and the Agony* (Harper Collins, 1992)
Omond, Roger *The Apartheid Handbook* (Penguin, 1986)
Smith, Susanna *Front Line Africa: the Right to a Future* (Oxfam, 1990)
Sparks, Alistair *The Mind of South Africa* (Mandarin, 1991)
UNICEF *Children on the Front Line: A Report for UNICEF* (UNICEF, 1989)

Personal accounts
Biko, Steve *Testimony of Steve Biko* (Heinemann Educational, 1979)
Mandela, Nelson *The Struggle is my Life* (International Defence and Aid Fund for Southern Africa, 1986)

Military and security issues
Cawthra, Gavin, *Brutal Force: The Apartheid War Machine* (International Defence and Aid fund for Southern Africa, 1986)
Cawthra, Gavin, *Peace and the Apartheid Police* (Catholic Institute for International Relations, 1992)

Novels
The subject of South Africa and apartheid has encouraged some powerful literature. A classic novel from the 1940s about apartheid is *Cry, the Beloved Country* by Alan Paton (Longman, 1986). For more recent works there are the novels of Nadine Gordimer such as *Essential Gesture* (Jonathan Cape, 1988), *My Son's Story* (Bloomsbury, 1990) and *Jump and other stories* (Bloomsbury, 1991). See also the work of Andre P Blink: *Actor's Terror* (Secker & Warburg, 1991) and *State of Emergency* (Fontana, 1989).

Films
Recent films covering the problems of apartheid are the well-known *Cry Freedom*, about the friendship between Black Consciousness activist Steve Biko and journalist Donald Woods and the problems created by the apartheid system; *A World Apart*, the life of the late Ruth First, the South African writer and anti-apartheid activist; *A Dry, White Season*, a film about a black South African in prison and his relationship with a white lawyer.

INDEX